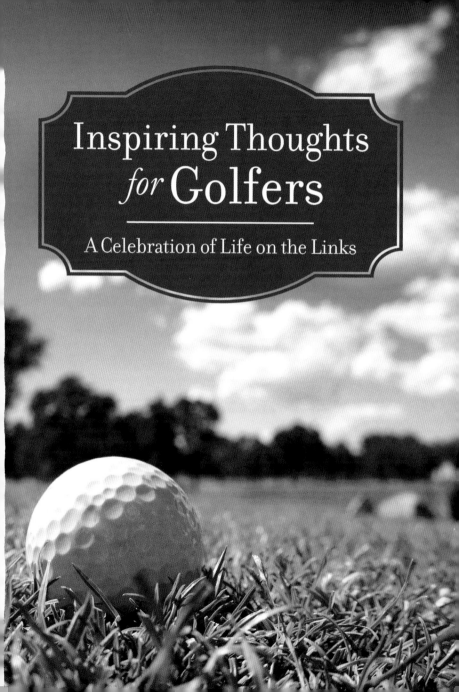

Inspiring Thoughts *for* Golfers

A Celebration of Life on the Links

Inspiring Thoughts
for Golfers

A Celebration of Life on the Links

BARBOUR
PUBLISHING

Lee Warren

ISBN 978-1-60260-750-7

Cover image: David H. Collier/Workbook Stock/Getty Images

Published by Barbour Publishing, Inc., P.O. Box 719, Uhrichsville, Ohio 44683, www.barbourbooks.com

Our mission is to publish and distribute inspirational products offering exceptional value and biblical encouragement to the masses.

Member of the
Evangelical Christian
Publishers Association

Printed in China.

Contents

INTRODUCTION:
What We Love About Golf

We golfers are in good company.

As the twenty-first century dawned, research showed that nearly thirty million Americans played golf at least once per year—with nearly a third of them labeled as "frequent" golfers. Nearly two million of us spend more than a hundred days on the links annually.

Of course, golf is played around the world, too—from Europe to Japan to South Africa—and watched by millions more on television. The old Scottish game has become a global, multibillion dollar industry.

But why? What is it that we love about golf?

More than any other sport, golf mingles the enjoyment of nature, the satisfaction of personal participation, the intrigue of a colorful past, and the fellowship of like-minded people. Those elements combine to create a real passion in many of us.

Those elements can also point us toward deeper spiritual truths in our lives. And that's what *Inspiring Thoughts for Golfers* is about—it's a celebration of the old game we love, the new thrill we get with every good shot, and the timeless God who watches over it all.

Being Outdoors

By the word of the LORD the heavens were made,
and by the breath of his mouth all their host.
He gathers the waters of the sea as a heap;
he puts the deeps in storehouses.
Let all the earth fear the LORD;
let all the inhabitants of the world
stand in awe of him!

PSALM 33:6–8

The term *links*, as it applies to golf, comes from the seaside sand hills of Scotland, where the game was born. Uneven fairways, thick roughs, and deep "pot bunkers" make a true links course challenging—as does the stiff breeze blowing in off the ocean.

But, oh, what an incredible setting for a few hours of play!

Surf, Sand, Scorecard

Few of us will ever have the privilege of playing a course like the Ailsa in Turnberry, Scotland. But we can always dream.

Situated on Scotland's west coast, overlooking the Irish Sea, Turnberry has humbled some of the world's best golfers. On the first day of the 1986 British Open, due to a combination of cold and wind, not even a single player was able to better par. In fact, the entire field was more than twelve hundred strokes over.

Locals say that if you can see Ailsa Craig—a volcanic rock island ten miles out in the Firth of Clyde—it's about to rain. If you can't see the island, it is raining.

But Turnberry's beauty more than makes up for the inconvenience of the weather. Ailsa's ninth hole, number nine on *Golf Magazine*'s list of the five hundred best in the world, is called "Bruce's Castle"

after the nearby ruins of the fourteenth-century hall of Scottish king Robert the Bruce. There's also a picturesque lighthouse in the distance.

Players tee off from an outcropping of rocks and must drive two hundred yards over ocean, beach, and massive stone in their attempt to complete the 454-yard hole in four strokes.

Think you could do that? It doesn't really matter. Wouldn't it be great just to be there?

*Praise the L*ORD *from the earth,*
you great sea creatures and all deeps,
fire and hail, snow and mist,
stormy wind fulfilling his word!
Mountains and all hills, fruit trees and all cedars!
Beasts and all livestock,
creeping things and flying birds!

P<small>SALM</small> 148:7–10

The floods have lifted up, O LORD,
the floods have lifted up their voice;
the floods lift up their roaring.
Mightier than the thunders of many waters,
mightier than the waves of the sea,
the LORD on high is mighty!

PSALM 93:3–4

Golf at the Water's Edge

The links aren't limited to Scotland.

California's Pebble Beach Golf Links, on the Pacific Ocean's Carmel Bay, boast plenty of surf, sand, and rock cliffs, too. Opened in 1919, its designer used a figure-eight layout to place as many of the holes as possible along the beautiful Monterey coastline.

Pebble Beach's par-5 eighteenth hole, *Golf Magazine*'s eighteenth best in the world, covers 543 yards and forces players to hug the ocean with their drives, avoid a few scenic but troublesome trees, and get past a large bunker fronting the green.

Unlike the nearby Cypress Point Golf Club, known for its exclusivity (comedian Bob Hope, himself a member, was quoted as saying, "One year they had a big membership drive at Cypress. They drove out forty members"), Pebble Beach is public. But be ready

to pay for the privilege of golfing in such beautiful surroundings—roughly five hundred dollars per round.

For other breathtaking oceanfront golfing, you might consider Oregon's Pacific Dunes, The Ocean Course at South Carolina's Kiawah Island, or California's Half Moon Bay Golf Links. And then there are those courses that overlook lakes, like northern Michigan's Bay Harbor Golf Club.

There's just something about water—from the endless oceans to that tiny, ball-eating pond—that adds to the golfing experience.

The Wonders of Water

Even before God created light, His spirit "was hovering over the face of the waters" of the newly created earth (Genesis 1:2).

On the second and third days of creation, God separated the waters on the earth from those in the sky and collected under the sky into seas. On the fifth day, He filled those seas with teeming creatures.

Water plays a prominent role throughout scripture. From Moses' parting of the Red Sea, to Joshua's crossing of the Jordan River, to Jesus' walking on the Sea of Galilee, to the apostle Paul's shipboard missionary journeys, many of the most familiar people and events of the Bible have connections to water.

And then there's the "living water" that Jesus promised a socially rejected woman at a well in Samaria. "Everyone who drinks of this water will be thirsty

18

again," Jesus told the woman, "but whoever drinks of the water that I will give him will never be thirsty again. The water that I will give him will become in him a spring of water welling up to eternal life" (John 4:13–14).

This spiritual water—cleansing, refreshing, life-giving—is free to anyone who will take it. "Whoever believes in me, as the Scripture has said, 'Out of his heart will flow rivers of living water,' " Jesus said in the book written by his close friend John, who explained, "Now this he said about the Spirit, whom those who believed in him were to receive" (John 7:38–39).

Next time you see water at the golf course—whether the surging sea, a placid pond, or a babbling brook—remember Jesus' "living water." And then drink deeply!

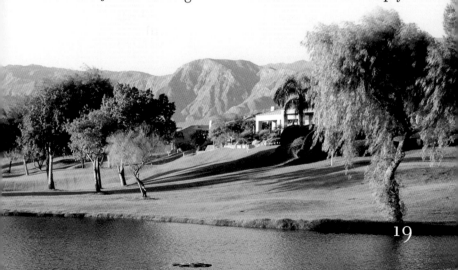

"Therefore they are before the throne of God, and serve him day and night in his temple; and he who sits on the throne will shelter them with his presence. They shall hunger no more, neither thirst anymore; the sun shall not strike them, nor any scorching heat. For the Lamb in the midst of the throne will be their shepherd, and he will guide them to springs of living water, and God will wipe away every tear from their eyes."

REVELATION 7:15–17

With as much as two-thirds of the land on golf courses considered "rough" or out-of-bounds, some proprietors are converting that land to natural habitats for wildlife. By limiting treatment and allowing trees and brush to grow naturally in such areas, they find the wildlife gladly making homes there.

A Bear of a Course

All sorts of wildlife call the Broadmoor East Course in Colorado Springs home. That's not a surprise, since it sits at the foot of the Rocky Mountains.

Golfers often play shots from hoof- and paw-prints left behind by deer, bobcats, mountain lions, and other creatures—since the standard rules of golf offer no relief for conditions caused by "non-burrowing" animals. But nobody—player or fan alike—was prepared for what happened at Broadmoor East during the 2008 U.S. Senior Open.

During the second round of play, an adult black bear wandered out of the mountains and onto the course. He (or she—apparently nobody got close enough to know for sure) ambled across several fairways on the back nine before crossing the forward

tee box on the fourteenth hole. Golfers, reporters, and onlookers steered clear, and the bear eventually made its way back into the wilderness.

"You don't get that every week," said John Cook, who shot a two-over-par 72 for the round. Leader Fred Funk, with a one-under-par 69, joked that Jack Nicklaus, "the Golden Bear," wasn't playing, "so I guess that's a substitute."

Though the strange event stirred up excitement, nobody—including the bear—was hurt. But everyone who was at Broadmoor East that day went home with some great stories to tell.

"Are not two sparrows sold for a penny? And not one of them will fall to the ground apart from your Father. But even the hairs of your head are all numbered. Fear not, therefore; you are of more value than many sparrows."

MATTHEW 10:29–31

According to the USGA Rule Book, a golfer receives relief if his or her ball ends up in an "abnormal ground condition" created by a burrowing animal. A "burrowing animal" is one that makes a hole for habitation or shelter, such as a groundhog, gopher, rabbit, or mole. Though dogs like to dig, they don't count.

A Different Kind of Birdie

TPC Sawgrass in Ponte Vedra Beach, Florida, is a beautiful golf course. Its signature hole, No. 17, is one of the most famous in golf. The 132-yard, par-3 is nearly surrounded by water and often referred to as the "island hole"—though technically it's a peninsula, since it's attached by an isthmus. But in 1998, the course and its seventeenth hole became famous for something else.

Competing in the Players Championship, Brad Fabel noticed a seagull sitting in front of the famed green. As he teed up, Fabel joked to himself that he might hit the bird with his shot and watch his ball end up in the water.

That didn't happen—but what did was even more amazing. Fabel's shot landed safely on the green, but caught the eye of the seagull. The gallery began to cheer, apparently thinking the bird might try to pick up the ball and fly away. That's exactly what happened, though the bird eventually dropped the ball into the water below.

Officials ruled that Fabel—now retired from playing and a rules official himself—should place the ball approximately where it was before the seagull got involved, without a penalty stroke.

Find the story hard to believe? You can easily find video on the Internet!

The Testimony of Wildlife

On the fifth day of creation, God created "living creatures according to their kinds—livestock and creeping things and beasts of the earth according to their kinds" (Genesis 1:24). Psalm 104:10 says that God makes "springs gush forth in the valleys," providing water to every beast while the birds sing in the branches of nearby trees (104:12).

The psalmist paints a beautiful picture, doesn't he? And it begs the question: If God is willing to do all of that for *animals*, how much more is He willing to do for us, people created in His own image?

God made and keeps wildlife for a variety of reasons, including to serve the needs of human beings. But consider how content the animals seem to be as they live their God-given lives. It's a testimony to us

of the good, gracious, and loving heavenly Father who made us, as well.

The next time you play a round of golf, pause to think of the animals on the course. Watch a squirrel scurry across the fairway. Marvel as birds fly overhead, chirping their praise to God. Listen to the sound of bullfrogs croaking in a nearby water hazard.

Sacred moments have less to do with hitting a perfect shot—and much more with being conscious of the holy, powerful, creator God.

*But God remembered Noah
and all the beasts and all the livestock
that were with him in the ark.
And God made a wind blow over the earth,
and the waters subsided.*

GENESIS 8:1

Friendly Competition

*Do you not know that in a race
all the runners run,
but only one receives the prize?
So run that you may obtain it.*
1 CORINTHIANS 9:24

Forget your opponents;
always play against par.
SAM SNEAD

Arnold Palmer vs. Jack Nicklaus

Arnold Palmer vs. Jack Nicklaus is number six on ESPN's "Ten Greatest Rivalries in Sports" list and number two (second only to *Tiger Woods vs. Old Man Time*) on Golf.com's "Ten Greatest Rivalries" roster—and with good reason. Palmer arrived on the golfing scene as a young, good-looking, charismatic guy loved by fans. Nicklaus came later as the talented challenger determined to overtake Palmer. It took fans longer to warm up to him, but their rivalry is often credited for bringing golf to the masses,

At the 1962 U.S. Open at Oakmont Country Club in Oakmont, Pennsylvania, the two were paired up for all four rounds. Excited fans saw Palmer and Nicklaus end up in a playoff, which Nicklaus won by three shots.

Although the two men competed fiercely, they also had a high level of respect for each other. Shortly after Nicklaus joined the PGA Tour, Palmer gave him a short-game lesson, advising him to putt from the fringe rather than chipping the ball. Nicklaus followed the advice and undoubtedly used it against Palmer at one time or another.

Some players need direct competitors to make them better. Others dislike such pressure and avoid the rivalries. Fans of golf can be thankful that Arnold Palmer and Jack Nicklaus challenged each other to better and better play. Because of that, we've enjoyed decades worth of world-class competition.

But in the end it's still a game of golf,
and if at the end of the day
you can't shake hands with your
opponents and still be friends,
then you've missed the point.
PAYNE STEWART

*Do nothing from rivalry or conceit,
but in humility count others
more significant than yourselves.*
PHILIPPIANS 2:3

Sam Snead vs. Ben Hogan

Sam Snead vs. Ben Hogan is third on Golf.com's list of the 10 greatest rivalries of the game. Hogan was known as an introvert, while Snead was outgoing. Hogan won the U.S. Open four times. Snead never took a U.S. Open, though he won more tournaments (82) than any other golfer in history. Hogan had a reputation as a hard worker, while Snead possessed such an easy swing some felt he was hardly trying.

Their rivalry is perhaps best remembered for their play at the Masters between 1949 and 1954. Hogan won the tournament in 1951 and '53, while Snead prevailed in '49, '52, and '54. The 1954 tournament featured a hard-charging amateur named

Billy Joe Patton who aced the par-3 sixth hole at the Augusta National Golf Club. When he faded on the back nine, Hogan and Snead ended up tied, headed for a playoff.

It was a classic battle for 18 holes. Snead and Hogan were tied after the first 9 holes. On the par-5 thirteenth, Hogan laid up on his second shot while Snead went for the green and made it. After Hogan three-putted the sixteenth, it was clear sailing for Snead, who won the Masters for his third and final time. Golf legend Bobby Jones called it the greatest championship he'd ever seen.

Respectful Rivals

In Matthew 22:39, Jesus told us to love our neighbors as ourselves. In the context of sport, some might say that it's impossible to be competitive and friendly at the same time. But there are two high school golf teams in Wisconsin who would say otherwise.

Kettle Moraine and Arrowhead high schools have two of the best boys' golf programs in the state. The nearby schools have been athletic rivals since 1966, and are each very open about how much they love to defeat the other school.

Chuck Delsman, who writes for the *Lake Country Reporter*, noted how the two teams ended up at the same hotel in 1999 for an out-of-town golf tournament. Coaches and team members began spending time with each other—and a bond developed. It didn't change the fact that each individual wanted to beat "the other

guys" on the golf course. But a genuine respect grew, so much so that each team roots for the other when they aren't competing head-to-head. And when they do play against each other, they respectfully lay it on the line.

The two teams' best players—Mike Sorenson of Arrowhead, and Sam Frank of Kettle Moraine—among others, battled it out for conference Player of the Year in 2009, with the nod going to Sorenson. It'll probably be a subject for discussion for years to come, since the two planned to become teammates at the University of Wisconsin.

*Do not rejoice when your enemy falls,
and let not your heart be glad when he stumbles,
lest the LORD see it and be displeased,
and turn away his anger from him.*
PROVERBS 24:17–18

According to the USGA rule book, the game relies on individuals to exhibit integrity toward one another. "All players should conduct themselves in a disciplined manner, demonstrating courtesy and sportsmanship at all times, irrespective of how competitive they may be. This is the spirit of the game of golf."

Integrity Matters

Wendy Ward joined the LPGA in 1996 and had two career titles before making a run at what would have been her first major title at the 2000 LPGA Championship in Wilmington, Delaware.

Ward was leading the tournament in the final round when she addressed her ball on the green at the thirteenth hole for an eight-foot putt to save par. After grounding her putter, she looked at the hole to line up her shot. Then she noticed that her ball had moved. She hadn't touched it—but the rules state that if a ball moves after it has been addressed, for any reason, the player receives a one-stroke penalty.

Nobody saw the ball move, but Ward knew it had—so she backed away from the putt and called for an official to explain what happened. Calling a one-stroke penalty on herself, Ward ended up missing a playoff that day

by a single shot. But she gained a lot more than a championship.

"The feedback that I received after that was phenomenal, and I knew that God's goodness was there," Ward told CBN.com afterward. "Despite the disappointment in not winning the event, there was such a greater story to be told."

Ward is a Christian, more concerned about her integrity and doing the right thing than with winning a tournament unfairly. As the Proverbs say, "whoever walks in integrity walks securely" (10:9).

The three things I fear most in golf are lightning,
Ben Hogan, and a downhill putt.

Sam Snead

Whatever you do, work heartily,
as for the Lord and not for men,
knowing that from the Lord you will receive
the inheritance as your reward.
You are serving the Lord Christ.
COLOSSIANS 3:23–24

Taking Responsibility

J. P. Hayes knows what it feels like to win a PGA Tour event. He's won two of them in his career. But that doesn't mean he has a ticket to play in every event. In fact, in 2008, Hayes finished outside the top 150 players on the money list, so he had to play in a qualifying tournament to get on the 2009 Tour.

During the second stage of the qualifier in Texas, Hayes's caddie gave him a ball for the twelfth hole, which Hayes hit from the tee then chipped onto the green. But when he marked his ball, Hayes saw it wasn't the same model he'd started the round with. Alerting an official to the rules violation, Hayes accepted a two-shot penalty.

By the end of the round, Hayes was still in a good position to advance to the final qualifying stage later in the year. But back in his hotel room, he began to

wonder if the ball he'd hit on No. 12 was on the USGA's approved list of balls. It wasn't. The mistake cost him a spot on the 2009 Tour.

Hayes didn't blame his caddie; instead, he took full responsibility for the errors.

He could have kept quiet, and nobody would have known. So why speak up? In an interview with ESPN, Hayes said, "I didn't feel like I had an option. We play by the rules and once I realized the ball was not on the conforming ball list, I was disqualified. I didn't need anybody to tell me that."

Living to Honor God's Name

Golf is the only major sport in which participants are expected to police their own actions on the field of play. Officials are not readily available during every shot on every hole. So the equipment in use, the scores that are recorded, the boundaries of each course, and other details of the game are subject to players being completely honest—even and *especially* when nobody else is watching. The integrity of the game is at stake.

If golfers are willing to honor such a high code of ethics for the game they love, how much more should Christians honor God in truthfulness? Shouldn't we be completely honest about our faults before Him, and strive to represent Him faithfully?

That's what David prayed in Psalm 69:5–6: "O God, you know my folly; the wrongs I have done are not hidden from you. Let not those who hope in you be put to shame through me, O Lord GOD of hosts; let not those who seek you be brought to dishonor through me, O God of Israel."

Imagine what life would be like if we lived all our days like a golfer of integrity—if we confessed every sin, if we were completely honest with God and our fellow man about our faults.

What if we were driven to do so because we wanted to see God and His name honored? How might that change the way we go about our everyday lives?

*An athlete is not crowned
unless he competes
according to the rules.*
2 TIMOTHY 2:5

History and Tradition

Remember the days of old;
consider the years of many generations;
ask your father, and he will show you,
your elders, and they will tell you.
DEUTERONOMY 32:7

The game of golf—in the quasi-form in which we know it, began in Scotland in the fifteenth century, although various forms of the game existed long before then in several European countries. Even the word *golf* has evolved. In the game's earliest forms it was referred to as *goff*, *gowf*, *golve*, or *kolf*.

DAVID STIRK
GOLF: THE HISTORY OF AN OBSESSION

The Royal and Ancient Golf Club

Golf existed for some time before the creation of the Society of St. Andrews Golfers in Scotland. But St. Andrews brought much of the structure and organization to the game that we know today.

In 1754, the twenty-two founders of St. Andrews created the following written statement (which can be found on the Web site of the St. Andrews Links Trust—an independent and charitable body that runs St. Andrews):

"The Noblemen and Gentlemen above named being admired of the Ancient and healthful exercise of the Golf, and at the same time having the interest and prosperity of the ancient city of St. Andrews at heart, being the Alma Mater of the Golf, did in the year of our Lord 1754 contribute for a Silver club having a St. Andrew engraved on the head thereof to be played for

on the Links of St. Andrews upon the fourteenth day of May said year, and yearly in time coming subject to the conditions and regulations following."

In 1834, with the influence of King William IV, the society became known as the Royal and Ancient Golf Club. By the turn of the twentieth century, "the R & A" had become the recognized authority of the game, developing a uniform set of rules that have evolved over time. Today the R & A governs all world golf except in the United States, where United States Golf Association has jurisdiction. But the two entities work together to make the rules of golf as uniform as possible.

Thus says the LORD: "Stand by the roads, and look, and ask for the ancient paths, where the good way is; and walk in it, and find rest for your souls."
JEREMIAH 6:16

In 1457, King James II prohibited golf in Scotland because it was too popular with his men. Seems they were neglecting their archery practice in favor of golf—leaving the country vulnerable to its enemies.

The PGA and LPGA

In January 1916, a group of golf professionals and top amateurs met for lunch in New York City at the invitation of department store magnate Rodman Wanamaker. He believed an association of professional golfers could lead to greater golf equipment sales—and on April 10 of that year, thirty-five charter members founded the PGA (Professional Golfers Association) of America.

By October of 1916, the first PGA Championship was held with Wanamaker donating a trophy and the winners' purse of $2,580. The Wanamaker trophy, called by that name, is still awarded to the winner of the tournament. The PGA of America now calls itself "the largest working sports organization in the world, comprised of more than 28,000 dedicated men and women promoting the game of golf to everyone, everywhere."

The LPGA (Ladies Professional Golf Association), meanwhile, was founded in 1950 with thirteen charter members. In its inaugural season, golfers competed in fourteen events, with total prize money of about fifty thousand dollars. Growing quickly in popularity, ABC broadcast the final round of the 1963 U.S. Women's Open—the first time a women's golf event was televised nationally. Through the years, LPGA players such as Nancy Lopez and Annika Sorenstam have become household names.

The LPGA Tour and the LPGA Teaching and Club Professionals (T&CP) describe themselves as "the backbone of what has become the premier women's professional sports organization in the world today."

Honoring Those Who Went Before

As golfers slip on the Green Jacket for winning the Masters or embrace the Claret Jug for taking the British Open—or when they accept any other prize for winning a golf tournament—most are mindful of the many golfers who went before them and set the stage for their success. In golf's early days, visionary people organized the game—and once it was established, great players drew the masses to the sport.

Tigers Woods is considered by many to be the best player of all time, though he says he doesn't accept that: Woods calls Jack Nicklaus the best. The last time Nicklaus won a major, the 1986 Masters, Woods was all of ten years old. But as a student of the game, Woods is quick to note that Nicklaus has won

more majors (eighteen) than anybody else—including Tiger's fourteen. Such humility only adds to the legacy of Woods and the game as a whole.

Is there a spiritual lesson to be learned here? How much more ought we to remember and honor faithful Christians who went before us? Many became martyrs for Christ, prompting Tertullian—a second-century theologian—to say, "The blood of the martyrs is the seed of the church."

Christ died for sins. Many believers in every century since have died for Christ—and many continue to do so around the world today. Why not take a moment to pray for them?

63

*So then, brothers, stand firm
and hold to the traditions
that you were taught by us,
either by our spoken word
or by our letter.*
2 THESSALONIANS 2:15

The trouble that most of us find
with the modern matched sets of clubs
is that they don't really seem to know
any more about the game
than the old ones did.

ROBERT BROWNING
A HISTORY OF GOLF

65

History of the Golf Ball

As far back as the sixteenth century, golf was played with a ball made of wood. Early in the seventeenth century, golfers used a ball of goose feathers wrapped in horse- or cowhide. To make a "feathery," all of the elements were assembled wet; when dry, the ball became hard. Since all featheries were made by hand, they were expensive—which made the sport less accessible for common people.

Things changed dramatically in the mid-1800s, when the Rev. Dr. Robert Adams Patterson devised the "guttie" ball made from the rubberlike sap (gutta-percha) of Malaysian trees. Gutties were much cheaper to produce, but their smooth surface made

them fly more poorly than the old featheries. So in the late 1800s, people began adding hand-hammered dimples for lift. Eventually, dimpled gutties were mass-produced, and the game grew in popularity.

By the early 1900s, golf balls were manufactured with a solid rubber core wrapped in thread. Greater yardage off the tee brought even more players to the links—and manufacturers have continued tinkering with the ball to meet the demands of a golfing public hungry for action. But the tinkering has its limits—the size and weight of golf balls are carefully regulated by both the R & A and the USGA.

Golf is a game whose aim
is to hit a very small ball
into an even smaller hole,
with weapons singularly
ill-designed for the purpose.
WINSTON CHURCHILL

My steps have held fast to your paths;
my feet have not slipped.
PSALM 17:5

History of the Golf Club

The earliest golf clubs were carved from wood. Over time, players turned to craftsmen for higher quality clubs that would lead to better scores—and, of course, a better chance of beating the competition.

King James IV is the first player known to have his own clubs specially made, by a bow maker in 1502. A predecessor, James II, had banned golf—but James IV reinstituted the game. Who could blame him?

Clubs began to evolve into "longnoses" for driving, "grassed drivers" for hitting long fairway shots, "spoons" for shorter shots, "niblicks" for chipping, and "cleeks" for putting.

Hardwoods were used for club heads, while the shafts were typically made of ash or hazel. Much like the first golf balls, early clubs were so expensive to

make that the average person couldn't afford them. In time, club makers began to experiment with other components—such as leather, bone fragments, metal, and hickory—in search of the ideal club.

Some changes were forced by the evolution of the golf ball. When "gutties" came along in the mid-1800s, longnoses were replaced with "bulgers," most similar to modern-day woods. By the early 1900s, steel-shafted clubs began to appear.

The 1960s and '70s brought even greater changes, which in turn brought even more people to the courses. Club head casting and graphite shafts still have an important place in the game in the twenty-first century.

A Golf Club Memorial

Shortly after my father died in 2000, my sister called to tell me that Dad's golf clubs were in her garage—and she thought I should be the one to get them. Starting when I was twelve, my dad and I spent many Saturday afternoons at the driving range and on various courses. He bought me my first set of clubs. He showed me how to grip a club, how to swing, and so much more.

Picking up his clubs and placing them in my car after he was gone was one of the hardest things I've ever done. But I also loved knowing that I would always have tangible reminders of the time we'd spent together.

I was now the proud owner of the 1-iron he could never hit and of the driver he used to crush balls off the tee. His golf bag was full of reminders of who he was—from the ball markers I remember seeing so many times to the tags he'd picked up at courses along

the way. It was also a reminder of who he was to me—a father who loved me enough to spend time with me.

Human beings need such reminders. In the Bible, God often called His people to build memorials out of tangible things (like rocks), so they would remember His faithfulness. You can find one such story in Genesis 28 when God promised to protect Jacob and to remain with him. Jacob took the stone he used as a pillow the night before and poured oil on it—setting it apart as a constant reminder of God's faithfulness.

Be imitators of me [Paul], as I am of Christ.
Now I commend you because
you remember me in everything
and maintain the traditions even as
I delivered them to you.
1 CORINTHIANS 11:1–2

Enjoying the Camaraderie

Iron sharpens iron,
and one man sharpens another.
PROVERBS 27:17

I have found the game to be,
in all factualness, a universal language
wherever I traveled at home or abroad.

BEN HOGAN

Arnold Palmer and Bob Hope

Shortly after Arnold Palmer won the 1954 U.S. Amateur tournament at the age of twenty-five, he received an invitation to appear on *The Bob Hope Show*. His appearance led to a friendship between the two men that lasted nearly fifty years. They played golf together, they acted together (Palmer was in a movie with Hope called *Call Me Bwana* in 1963), and they even spent some time together visiting President Nixon to talk about the Vietnam War.

The pair seemed to bring out the best in each other. When they were entertaining, Hope made Palmer look like a comedian, and when they were on the golf course, Palmer brought out the best in Hope's game.

An article on the *Golf Digest* Web site, "Friendship Links Palmer and Hope," recounted one of their

exchanges on *The Bob Hope Show*: "When Hope asked on one show, 'How come you never invited me to appear on 'Challenge Golf'?' Palmer replied, 'We don't do comedy, Bob.' When Hope explained, 'I mean to play golf,' Palmer deadpanned, 'We don't do comedy, Bob.' "

Palmer and Hope will always be known for the Bob Hope Desert Classic—a celebrity pro-am event. Palmer has been involved in the event since 1960 and has won it five times. The tournament has distributed some fifty million dollars to various charities. Bob Hope died in 2003 at the age of one hundred, but Arnold Palmer continues to carry the torch for his friend by hosting what is now called the Bob Hope Classic.

Love one another with brotherly affection.
Outdo one another in showing honor.
ROMANS 12:10

*A friend loves at all times,
and a brother is born for adversity.*
PROVERBS 17:17

Phil Mickelson and Fred Couples

The 2006 Masters will be remembered for Phil Mickelson winning the tournament for the second time. But it should be recalled for something else, as well—two top-notch competitors who laughed, joked, and inspired one another to be even better than they already were.

Going into the fourth round, Mickelson was one stroke ahead of Chad Campbell and Fred Couples. At the age of forty-six, Couples was trying to become the oldest man ever to win the Masters. Birdying the first hole, Couples shared the lead with Mickelson. The two friends, who happened to be playing together, walked from hole to hole smiling. Couples said afterward that they began to tell each other, "Let's make birdies"—and they did.

On the 510-yard thirteenth hole, Couples hit his tee

shot into a ditch. He pitched into the fairway, hit an iron to the green, then sank a 15-foot putt for birdie. Mickelson, meanwhile, was on in two and two-putted for birdie. Laughing, Mickelson told Couples, "I know we said 'Let's make birdies,' but let's make them the conventional way."

On No. 14, Couples—down by two strokes at the time—missed a four-foot birdie putt and the tournament slipped away from him. Mickelson went on to win, defeating Tim Clark by two shots, and Couples and four other players by three. Whatever the final standings, Mickelson and Couples proved that athletes can compete at the highest level while also enjoying each other's company.

Face-to-Face

Modern guys are probably more open to honest conversations with one another than in generations past—but it can still be awkward. Oftentimes, even when we do converse, we use gadgets of some sort to have the conversation. But gadgets can never replace simple face-to-face, or shoulder-to-shoulder, conversations. See how Exodus 33:11 describes the relationship that Moses and God had: "Thus the LORD used to speak to Moses face to face, as a man speaks to his friend."

Throughout the book of Exodus, you'll see God talking with Moses. In Exodus 3, the Lord manifested Himself as a burning bush, telling Moses to set His people free from the bondage they faced in Egypt. In Exodus 9, God urged Moses to confront Pharaoh. In Exodus 19:19, God spoke to Moses in thunder. And

in Exodus 20, God spoke to Moses on Mt. Sinai as He issued the Ten Commandments. A holy God was still interacting with Moses "face-to-face."

If you find yourself needing time with an old friend, golf may be your answer. Several hours in a golf cart makes for a perfectly nonthreatening setting to discuss life. Give it a try—you'll probably both find it encouraging.

*For this is the message
that you have heard from the beginning,
that we should love one another.*
1 JOHN 3:11

If you think it's hard to meet new people,
try picking up the wrong golf ball.
JACK LEMMON

Friends Helping Friends

Bruce Edwards was more than just a caddy to Tom Watson. For nearly three decades, they worked as a team to win golf tournaments, each man doing what he did best—and off the course, seeing each other through the difficult moments of life.

Early in 2003, Edwards began to slur his words. Diagnosed with ALS (more commonly known as Lou Gehrig's Disease), he was told he had one to three years to live. But for the 2003 U.S. Open, Edwards chose to do what came naturally to him—he was on Watson's bag. Watson shot a five-under-par 65 in the first round, taking a share of the lead. The gallery cheered wildly as Watson and Edwards walked up the eighteenth fairway together. Ultimately, Watson didn't win the tournament—but he was more resolved than ever to help fight ALS for his friend and his friend's legacy.

At one point, Watson donated a million dollars of his winnings to ALS research.

Edwards died on April 8, 2004, the morning the Masters tournament began. Beforehand, Edwards told Watson to make sure he used the yardage book he'd kept for Watson because it included all of the layups. Watson had the book with him the day he learned of Edwards' death. Though physically apart, they were still together at the end.

A man of many companions
may come to ruin,
but there is a friend
who sticks closer than a brother.
PROVERBS 18:24

Golf is like fishing and hunting.
What counts is the companionship
and fellowship of friends,
not what you catch or shoot.
GEORGE ASHER

Continuing a Legacy

Sports Illustrated called LPGA golfer Heather Farr one of the game's most promising stars—and justifiably so. At the age of seventeen, she won the 1982 U.S. Girls' Junior Golf Championship. Two years later, she took the U.S. Women's Amateur Public Links title. By 1986, she was a member of the LPGA—but three years after that, at the age of twenty-four, she was diagnosed with breast cancer. She battled the disease—undergoing numerous medical procedures—before dying in 1993 at the age of twenty-eight. Her life may have been short, but she built lasting friendships on the tour.

The night she died, more than a dozen LPGA golfers were with Farr at the hospital. One of the last things Farr told a friend, fellow LPGA golfer Val Skinner, was that they really needed to warn young women of the risks of breast cancer. Skinner didn't forget her

friend's words. The Val Skinner Foundation has gone on to raise more than four million dollars for breast cancer education and research. She set up the LPGA Pros in the Fight to Eradicate Breast Cancer (LIFE) with proceeds going to Susan G. Komen for the Cure, the Cancer Institute of New Jersey (CINJ), and the Young Survival Coalition.

Skinner continues to honor her friend by telling Heather's story—about her vibrant fight and about her concern for the health of other women.

Jonathan and David

There's a common thread in the stories of Arnold Palmer and Bob Hope, Phil Mickelson and Fred Couples, Tom Watson and Bruce Edwards, and Heather Farr and Val Skinner. We see one person loving another and placing the other person's interest above his or her own. We see their sacrifices for one another, their laughter with one another, and sometimes their tears for one another.

Their friendships look a lot like the biblical relationship between Jonathan and David. Read 1 Samuel 18:1–3: "As soon as he [David] had finished speaking to Saul, the soul of Jonathan was knit to the soul of David, and Jonathan loved him as his own soul. And Saul took him that day and would not let him return to his father's house. Then Jonathan made a covenant with David, because he loved him as his own soul."

That friendship was soon to be tested. When Saul saw that God was with David, he wanted to kill his son's friend. David was a threat to Saul's throne, and the king wouldn't stand for it. What Saul didn't understand was the strength of the bond between Jonathan and David—it was so powerful that Jonathan was willing to defy his own father by informing David of Saul's plan to kill him.

That's what friendship looks like—overcoming evil with good. It is not self-seeking, but always more concerned with the welfare of the other person.

Do you have a friend like that in your life? If so, maintain the relationship. If not, be a friend to someone in need. You'll be glad you did.

*Bear one another's burdens,
and so fulfill the law of Christ.*
GALATIANS 6:2